SHIRLEY CHISHOLM IS A VERB!

written *by* **VERONICA CHAMBERS**

illustrated *by* **RACHELLE BAKER**

Dial Books for Young *Readers*

Some words, when they **CONNECT** with the right people, become almost like potions or spells. These words become magical.

That's the way it was with Congresswoman Shirley Chisholm and verbs. She understood, almost intuitively, how and why verbs are not just words about being, but doing.

Verbs are words that move the world forward.

Shirley's family understood
all about moving.

Her mother was from
Barbados, an island in
the Caribbean.

Her father was from
Guyana, a country in
South America.

They **MOVED** to
New York City, where
Shirley was born.

When Shirley was three, her mother sent her and her sisters to Barbados so that their parents could work more hours.

Her mother cleaned houses and office buildings. Her father worked in a factory. They worked all day and all night because they DREAMED of buying a home for their family in the United States.

In Barbados, surrounded by her grandmother, aunts, and uncles, little Shirley worked hard too.

Her classroom was noisy and the three teachers that shared the room needed to project to be heard above all of the passionate students.

But her teachers taught Shirley how to **SPEAK** up, and they helped her understand the power of words.

Later she would say, "If I speak and read and write easily, that early education is the cause."

When she was nine, Shirley and her sisters moved back from Barbados to Brooklyn. Everything in Brooklyn was different and Shirley missed the warm island weather.

But Shirley **LOVED** indoor activities like going to the movies and reading. Shirley was a voracious reader, much like her father.

Shirley was also a dedicated student and at her high school in Brooklyn, she was vice president of the Junior Arista Honor Society and **GRADUATED** with a medal of excellence in French. She earned scholarships to both Vassar and Oberlin Colleges, but her parents could not afford the room and board. Shirley decided to go to Brooklyn College instead and live at home in the brownstone her parents were ultimately able to buy through their hard work.

In college, Shirley decided to pursue a career in education.

She became a nursery school teacher, and then earned her master's degree.

Completing her education was hard work, but it paid off! She directed daycare centers and became a consultant to the city on early education. She helped implement and **ORGANIZE** a program called Head Start, which helps three- and four-year-olds get ready for kindergarten.

But Shirley wanted to help even more people. She believed that "Service to others is the rent you pay for your room on earth."

Which is another way to say that she wanted to use her verbs and **IMPROVE** the lives of as many people as she could, just like her parents and her teachers had improved her own.

She decided to go into politics. She ran for, and won, a seat on the New York State Assembly. The assembly makes decisions for people all over the state of New York.

She was one of the first people to argue that the New York State literacy test not be conducted only in English. New York was home to people from all over the world and Shirley thought it was important to **HONOR** the native languages of all the state's citizens.

For her work in the New York State government, she was awarded a "Salute to Women Doers" award.

She was always a doer.

Then, Shirley ran for the United States Congress, the part of the government that makes decisions for people all over the country.

It was a race few thought she could win. But Shirley believed if your heart told you it was the right thing to do, you should always **LISTEN.**

She knew she could only fail if she didn't try.

She **CAMPAIGNED**, meaning that she encouraged people to vote for her. Her slogan was: Unbought and Unbossed.

She wanted the people to know that she would never choose money or power over what was important to them.

She campaigned in both English and Spanish, because she wanted as many people as possible to understand her message.

In her speeches, she called herself "Fighting Shirley Chisholm" because she wanted voters to know she wasn't afraid to stand up for what she believed in.

The people of Brooklyn chose Shirley to **REPRESENT** them!
She became the first Black woman ever elected to Congress.

Shirley **TRAVELED** to Washington, DC.

There wasn't a single person who looked like her.

It was a lonely time.

Being the first and only often is.

But Shirley Chisholm wouldn't give up.

She thought of all the people back in Brooklyn who had **VOTED** for her.
Shirley felt forever linked to them.

Shirley's first assignment in Congress was the House Agriculture Committee, a group of people who **OVERSEE** the farmlands of America.

Shirley was disappointed. She came from a big city. How would working with farms help the people in Brooklyn who voted for her?

She shared this question with her friend. He encouraged her to use her position on the committee to help feed the hungry all over. Including her beloved Brooklyn.

Shirley helped to initiate a program called WIC, which assists Women, Infants, and Children in need of food.

Shirley also helped **CREATE** the national school lunch program, but she didn't decide the menus. (So if you don't like your lunch, please don't blame her!)

Because of her hard work, she eventually **EARNED** her dream job helping students and workers through the Education and Labor Committee.

Shirley said, "You don't make progress by standing on the sidelines, whimpering and complaining."

She said, "If they don't give you a seat at the table, bring a folding chair."

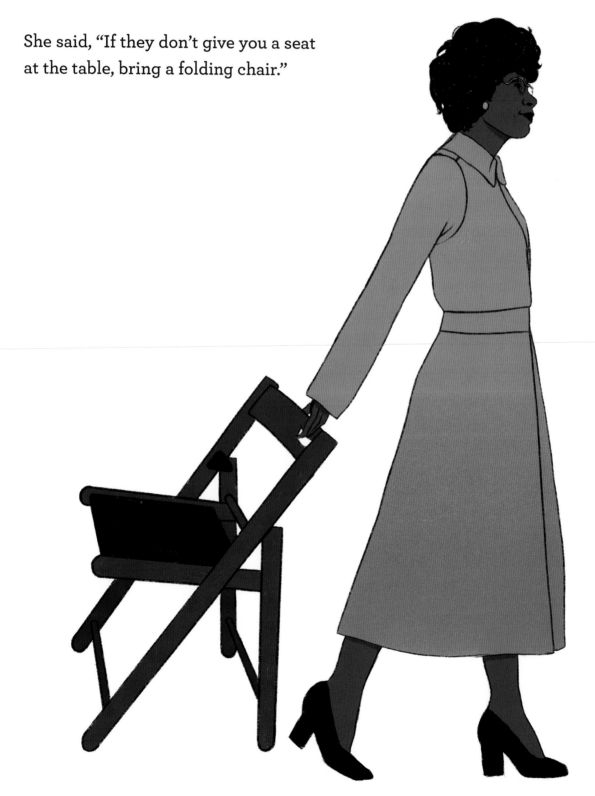

And Shirley wasn't just concerned about getting a seat at the table for herself. She never wanted to be the one and the only.

She **HELPED** create the Congressional Black Caucus so more African Americans could be elected to serve in Washington, DC. She wanted Congress to look like the America that had elected her.

Not everyone in Washington applauded Shirley's wins. She was always more interested in serving people than in making laws that helped big businesses.

The men on Capitol Hill who cared more about power and money said, "Go home, Shirley Chisholm."

She replied, "I'm Fighting Shirley Chisholm. You can't wish me away. You just can't."

She remembered her impassioned teachers and her hard-working parents and it gave her "the spirit and the spunk to CHALLENGE the age-old traditions." She said, "I'm not afraid of anything or anybody."

Shirley was so unafraid that in 1972, after four years in Congress, she decided to run for president! Before a large crowd of people she **ANNOUNCED**, "I stand before you today as a candidate for the presidency of the United States of America."

She was the first Black person, and the first woman, to make a serious bid for the presidency.

She said, "I am not the candidate for black America, although I am Black and proud."

"I am not the candidate of the women's movement of this country, although I am a woman and I am equally proud of that."

"I am the candidate of the people of America."

Shirley crisscrossed the nation, giving speeches, debating candidates on television, and registering voters. She needed to CONVINCE the Democratic Party that she would be the best candidate for president.

People had called Shirley Chisholm many things before, but now they said she was:

Black. Beautiful. Brave. Brainy. Bright. Believable.

Some of the other candidates were
angry that Shirley was taking votes
away from them. But Shirley knew
how to hold her ground. She said:

"Excuse me!
    I have a right to be here."

"Pay attention! I've got
    something to say."

"Listen! I've got a job to do
and I intend to **DO** it."

When people tried to silence her, Shirley spoke louder.

When the media ignored her, Shirley **PROTESTED** vigorously.

When other politicians tried to bully her, Shirley stood stronger.

When her opponents said hurtful things, Shirley smiled wider.

Then Shirley heard that the Democrats had decided that she would not be their presidential candidate. Shirley was disappointed, but not discouraged.

Shirley realized that just because she didn't win, it didn't mean that she lost.

During her presidential bid, she had **GAINED** more delegates than many in the party expected.

With each delegate that voted for her, she put a crack in the ceiling that separated women and men of color from the highest seat in the nation: the presidency.

Some races are relays. We only need to run as far and as fast as we can.

Shirley's verbs, her words, and her actions **PLANTED** the seeds of possibility for others.

Twelve years later, Geraldine Ferraro would crack the ceiling further when she gained the Democratic nomination for vice president.

Twenty-five years after that, President Barack Obama would **ASCEND** all the way to the White House.

Seven years later, Hillary Rodham Clinton would put eighteen million more cracks in that ceiling when the Democrats nominated her for president.

And then, in 2018, a record-breaking 131 women were elected to Congress. It is a number that would have made Shirley beam.

Part of the congressional class of 2018 was a young woman named Alexandria Ocasio-Cortez. Like Shirley, she was also known as the "Congresswoman from New York."

Like Shirley, Alexandria did things her way. And she prioritized the people who had elected her and put their concerns first.

Shirley Chisholm INSPIRED her.

On her first day in Congress, Alexandria said, "From suffragettes to Shirley Chisholm, I wouldn't be here if it wasn't for the mothers of the movement."

She informed the people in Washington that, in the spirit of Shirley, she was Fighting Alexandria and they couldn't just wish her away. They couldn't.

Shirley Chisholm once said, "The next time a woman of whatever color, or a dark-skinned person of whatever sex aspires to be president, the way should be a little smoother because I helped PAVE it."

It was always her intention to throw the doors of government wide open—and she did!

When Shirley retired from Congress, after serving seven consecutive terms in office, she said she wanted to be known for her courage to stand up for herself and the people who had elected her. She said, "I'd like them to say that Shirley Chisholm had guts."

In 2015, President Barack Obama **AWARDED** Chisholm the Medal of Freedom. Shirley's great-nephew accepted the award on her behalf. Speaking of her service to the nation, and how tireless she was in her quest, President Obama said, "There are people in our country's history who don't look left or right, they look straight ahead. Shirley Chisholm was one of those people."

Shirley Chisholm accomplished so much, because she chose her verbs carefully:

LEARN.

Negotiate.

Listen.

Stand.

CAMPAIGN.

Invite.

DEBATE.

Inspire.

Speak.

REPRESENT.

It's your turn now.
What verbs will you CHOOSE?

A personal note from the author

I grew up in Brooklyn and I remember walking to school and seeing Shirley Chisholm for Congress posters all around my neighborhood. We didn't have much money. There were days when my mother would announce that dinner would be some semblance of scraps from the pantry, what she called "air pudding and nothing pie."

And yet because of Shirley Chisholm, I thought, "I could be a congresswoman." After all, I passed a picture of a woman who looked a lot like me, who had that job.

I know that I'm not the only kid from the boroughs of New York who felt that way, because as I was growing up, I would hear Shirley Chisholm name-checked in the hip-hop songs that I loved. Like Biz Markie's lines "Make you cooperate with the rhythm/that is what I give them/Reagan is the president/But I voted for Shirley Chisholm."

She ran in 1972, but rapper after rapper cited her run many years later. Tribe Called Quest rapped, "I got a brave heart like the one called Shirley Chisholm." Redman and Method Man did a spin on Biz Markie's lines when they rapped, "Clinton is the president, but I voted for Shirley Chisholm." And I always loved the poetic elegance of Andre 3000's reference to her, "You're the prism/Shirley Chisholm/the first."

In 2004, an extraordinary young filmmaker named Shola Lynch debuted her wonderful documentary about Shirley's historic race, *Chisholm '72: Unbought & Unbossed*. In fact, it was a line from Ms. Lynch that inspired the title of this book!

Shirley Chisholm died just a few months later on January 1, 2005.

Lynch's documentary was nominated for a Sundance Grand Jury prize, won the Peabody Award, and is available on Amazon and Netflix. It is 77 minutes of inspiring American history with great clips featuring everyone from Walter Cronkite to Gloria Steinem to Shirley herself.

Shirley's autobiographies *The Good Fight* and *Unbought and Unbossed* are inspiring portraits of this one-of-a-kind civic leader.

If you are thinking about running for office, any kind of office, some websites you might want to consider are sheshouldrun.org, higherheightsforamerica.org, and runforsomething.net. There are lots of other ways to get involved, too—like volunteering for a campaign in your community, or a cause that's important to you. I hope this book inspires you to raise your voice, take charge, and make waves in support of the causes and leaders you believe in.

Verbs are words that show an action, occurrence, or state of being.
The words highlighted throughout this book are verbs that Shirley Chisholm
used and embodied to make the world a better place.

To Professor Alfred Rowe, who provided the batteries — V.C.

*To Bridgette and Tonyce, who taught me to always stand tall, put my foot
down, and keep my head up, even when it all feels impossible — R.B.*

Dial Books for Young Readers
An imprint of Penguin Random House LLC, New York

Text copyright © 2020 by Veronica Chambers
Illustrations copyright © 2020 by Rachelle Baker

Visit us online at penguinrandomhouse.com

Library of Congress Cataloging-in-Publication Data
Names: Chambers, Veronica, author. | Baker, Rachelle, illustrator.
Title: Shirley Chisholm is a verb / written byVeronica Chambers ; illustrated by Rachelle Baker.
Description: New York : Dial Books for Young Readers, [2020] | Audience: Ages 4–8 | Audience: Grades 2–3
| Summary: "A picture book biography celebrating the life and contributions of Shirley Chisholm, the first Black woman
in Congress, who sought the Democratic nomination to be the president of the United States"—Provided by publisher.
Identifiers: LCCN 2019054537 (print) | LCCN 2019054538 (ebook) | ISBN 9780803730892 (hardcover) | ISBN 9780593111079 (ebook)
| ISBN 9780593111086 (kindle edition) | Subjects: LCSH: Chisholm, Shirley, 1924–2005—Biography—Juvenile literature. | African
American women—Biography—Juvenile literature. | Legislators—United States—Biography—Juvenile literature. | Presidential
candidates—United States—Biography—Juvenile literature. | Teachers—United States—Biography—Juvenile literature. | United States.
Congress. House—Biography—Juvenile literature. | Classification: LCC E840.8.C48 C43 2020 (print) | LCC E840.8.C48 (ebook)
| DDC 328.73/092 [B]— dc23 | LC record available at https://lccn.loc.gov/2019054537
LC ebook record available at https://lccn.loc.gov/2019054538

Shirley Chisholm photograph (page 39) courtesy of Mike Lien © 2020 The New York Times Company

Manufactured in China
ISBN 9780803730892

10 9 8 7 6 5 4 3 2 1

Design by Jennifer Kelly
Text set in Archer

The art in this book was created digitally with Procreate on an iPad Pro, and with the help of countless cups of Earl Grey tea and biscoff cookies.